The Pound Cake
COOKBOOK

by

Bibb Jordan

To Chris and Chuck, loyal testers,
and to El, who always says, "More chocolate!"

≈ ♦ ≈

Published by LONGSTREET PRESS, INC.,
a subsidiary of Cox Newspapers,
a division of Cox Enterprises, Inc.
2140 Newmarket Parkway
Suite 118
Marietta, Georgia 30067

Copyright © 1994 by Bibb Jordan

Printed in the United States of America

1st printing, 1994

ISBN: 1-56352-107-5

This book was printed by Horowitz/Rae Book Manufacturers, Inc., Fairfield, New Jersey

Cover painting by B. Gail Smith
Jacket and book design by Laura McDonald

Contents

❧ ♦ ❧

Introduction

❧ ✦ ❧

There is hardly another American dessert that is thought of as nostalgically as a golden, buttery pound cake. It's the cake people most often remember having eaten at their grandmother's house or at church socials; the one they paid a nickel a slice for at school bake sales and that they brought along with fried chicken and potato salad on picnics; the one that was always set out on the buffet table with all the more holiday-oriented desserts at Thanksgiving and Christmas; the one their mother baked for the family of someone who was sick or who had just had a baby.

Part of the reason for pound cakes' popularity comes from the fact they keep well (often even improving in flavor after a day or two), they can be made without a lot of fuss or bother or expensive ingredients, and they don't have to be dressed up with icing to stay moist or be considered special. And, there's nothing quite like walking into a house where a pound cake has just been baked — the aroma is incredible.

Pound cakes are relatively simple cakes that traditionally called for a pound of butter, a pound of sugar, a pound of eggs, and a pound of flour. Although the amounts of those ingredients have certainly changed over the years, the same four basic ingredients still characterize a pound cake (only the seasonings and flavorings change), and nearly all pound cakes are made following the same standard procedure of creaming the butter and sugar, adding the eggs, and then carefully mixing in the flour and flavorings.

Yet, as popular and as supposedly simple as pound cakes are, few cooks have more than one really good recipe. A local newspaper's food editor said that recipes for pound cakes were the ones most requested by that paper's readers, which indicates that not that many cooks were all that pleased with the one or two recipes they had. Some people also tended to be pretty "loose" when it came to defining what they actually served as a pound cake (there's one member of the Jordan family who calls anything larger than a donut that still has a hole in the middle of it, a "pound cake").

Few cakes, however, seem to evoke as much satisfaction as the memory of some long ago slice of moist and buttery, velvet-textured cake baked by a grandmother or housekeeper or much-loved aunt. In fact, it became the *idea* of a pound cake that was perfect in most people's minds.

Therefore, my objective was to find pound cakes that were as good as their memory, cakes that came out perfectly every time.

Well, there weren't that many of them in the beginning. No matter how many recipes I pored over or how many cakes I baked, I found very few that weren't lacking in some way. Some smelled great and looked wonderful, but fell apart in my hands. Others were way too dry. Two or three would have served nicely if I had needed a really big pencil eraser, or a door stop, or an anchor, but they didn't do much for me when all I really wanted was just a good piece of cake. And even those recipes that I counted as successful — meaning they had great taste, smooth texture, wonderful smell — rarely seemed very different from hundreds of others just like them.

Why weren't there more pound cakes with nuts? With fruits? Why not more than just one or two basic chocolates? To find out, I began to experiment, adding flavorings and ingredients that I felt complemented one another. Very quickly I learned that for every success, I could count on a garbage can full of failures. I learned that it is fairly easy to add flavorings and ingredients to a regular cake but less easy when you're making a true pound cake because few can stand up under the length of cooking time required and it is difficult to create a batter that can support heavy ingredients. I learned that chocolate pound cakes are easy to over-cook. I learned that I don't ever want to see another straw-berry pound cake as long as I live (suffice it to say that there is a *reason* why there aren't any famous ones in the world!). I learned that creating new and different pound cakes is hard work. And I learned that there's a double meaning to the term *pound* cake: if you bake as many as I did, you're going to waddle away from the project with a few extra pounds on the haunches. I promise.

But I also promise this: the pound cakes that I finally considered good enough to include in this book are terrific. I have my per-sonal favorites (as do the family members and friends who helped taste so many different cakes during the nearly three years it took to finish this book), but they're *all* wonderful, and they all work if you follow the exact cooking times and oven tem-peratures and use the exact measurements and ingredients that are listed in each recipe.

There are secrets, of course, to making really good pound cakes. Most are baking fundamentals, known to those who bake often; but a few are ones I discovered after countless trials and errors. Those secrets are listed on the following pages and are worth the reading.

In all cases I stuck with the basic procedure for making pound cakes: creaming the butter and sugar, adding the eggs, and then carefully mixing in the flour and flavorings.

Coming up with a really good basic chocolate pound cake was one of the more difficult challenges of this book. There just weren't many that reminded me of what I'd had as a child. Finally, I created two basic ones — Buttermilk Chocolate Pound Cake and Chocolate Walnut Pound Cake — that have the kind of flavor I remember from so many years ago and that everyone agrees are wonderful. Chocolate Chip Cookie Pound Cake and Oreo Pound Cake were created especially for children, although grownups eat them with equal enthusiasm. Mocha Pound Cake with Coffee Creme Anglaise was designed for adult chocolate lovers with a slightly more sophisticated taste. And the Chocolate Truffle Pound Cake is, well, truly remarkable.

THE POUND CAKE COOKBOOK includes something for nearly every taste, including the Low Cholesterol Poppy Seed Pound Cake (even though "low-cholesterol pound cake" is an oxymoron if there ever was one). In most cases the recipes call for ingredients that are readily available, and I tried to create cakes that could be made without spending all day in the kitchen or breaking the budget. Some of the cakes obviously, though, are for special occasions and are proof that pound cakes don't have to be plain and simple. But don't tell your grandmother.

Secrets to the
Perfect Pound Cake

❧ ✦ ❧

The following techniques will provide help with the baking problems most commonly associated with pound cakes.

CAKE PANS ❧

One of the most important aspects of baking is using the proper pan. Always use the exact size and type of pan the recipe calls for. A pan that is too large does not provide the proper support and will not allow the cake to rise properly, and one that is too small will cause the batter to overflow.

Cake pans that have white interiors do not work well. Often the bottom of the cake does not brown at all, and sometimes the cake is even slightly soggy. Therefore, it is best to use cake pans with dark or metal interiors. Some tube pans have dark interiors, and nearly all bundt pans do.

Unless the recipe states otherwise, prepare the pans for baking by thoroughly rubbing the inside walls, the bottom, and tube (in a bundt or tube pan) with softened butter. Then toss a small amount of flour around the insides of the pan to coat completely. To make sure the tube is successfully covered, it is sometimes helpful to put a small amount of flour in a sifter and shake over the tube.

This traditional method of greasing and flouring does not work well with the bundt-lette pans (see recipes on pages 79-89). For these types of pans, use a vegetable oil-based non-stick cooking spray such as Pam or Baker's Joy.

BUTTER ∾

For all cakes in this cookbook, use only butter that is labeled "unsalted." Unless the recipe states otherwise, bring the butter to room temperature by removing from the refrigerator and placing on the counter for one hour. (If you forget this step, be *extremely* careful trying to soften butter in a microwave or on top of the stove; you absolutely *cannot* use melted butter for the cake batter, and even butter that has been overly softened will start to break down and won't incorporate as much air, greatly affecting the success of the cake.)

SUGARS ∾

When the recipe calls for "sugar," this refers to regular white, granulated sugar.

Confectioners' sugar, used most often in sauces and frostings or for dusting, is sometimes referred to as "powdered sugar." Granulated sugar and confectioners' sugar should only be used as specified in each recipe.

Brown sugars are referred to as "light brown" and "dark brown" and should be used according to the recipe and not replaced by one another. They too should be used only when called for and not used in place of granulated sugar. Brown sugar has a decidedly different weight and texture from granulated sugar; therefore, when measuring brown sugar do not measure it loosely but "pack" it with the back of a spoon into the measuring cup. After a box or bag of brown sugar has been opened, it should be stored in an airtight container or zip-lock plastic bag to keep it soft and fresh.

CREAMING BUTTER AND SUGAR ∽

For these dense butter cakes, aeration is extremely important and it is in the creaming of the butter and sugar that the most air is incorporated into the batter to create a light texture.

To successfully accomplish this important step, place the *room temperature* butter in a clean, dry bowl. Begin softening the butter by beating at medium speed with an electric mixer. Gradually add the sugar and beat at medium speed for several minutes, or until the mixture has become light and fluffy and reaches a pale color.

EGGS ∽

The size of eggs varies tremendously and therefore can change the amount of liquid in the batter. For the recipes in this book, all eggs used are those graded "large."

The eggs should be at room temperature (unless the recipe states otherwise) when added to the batter. This means taking the eggs from the refrigerator approximately one hour before using them. However, be careful not to leave them unrefrigerated for longer than an hour because of the threat of spoiling.

It is best to crack each egg individually into a small bowl or measuring cup to make sure the egg is fresh and that there is no shell accidentally poured into the batter. Add each egg one at a time to the batter and mix according to the recipe.

MIXING ∾

It is difficult to overbeat the butter and sugar. But by the time the flour and other dry ingredients have been added, you want to mix *only* enough to blend all the ingredients and have them incorporated well with one another. At this point, do not continue mixing more than necessary; overbeating can cause large air pockets, or tunneling, to form and make the texture of the finished cake tough.

FLOUR ∾

When the recipe calls for "flour," this refers to regular all-purpose flour. If self-rising or cake flour are called for, use accordingly, but make sure you do not replace one for another (which would more than likely result in a ruined cake). Any brand name of all-purpose flour can be used, but White Lily is an excellent flour and was one used with the most success when testing the recipes in this book.

When measuring flour, do not pour or pack the flour, but gently scoop the proper size measuring cup into the flour and lift out. With the straight edge of a knife or metal spatula, scrape off any excess flour.

If the recipe calls for "3 cups flour, sifted", this means to accurately measure the flour first, then sift into a large bowl. If it calls for "3 cups sifted flour", this means to sift the flour onto a clean surface or waxed paper and then gently spoon into the appropriate measuring cups and level with a knife or spatula.

CITRUS RIND OR ZEST ∽

Many of the recipes in this book call for grated lemon or orange rind or "zest." For zest, carefully grate the surface of a clean, dry lemon or orange, making sure to grate only the yellow outer rind (the white, pithy part of the rind can be bitter and alter the taste). For planning purposes, remember that it may take as many as three or four lemons, depending on their size, to get one full tablespoon of zest.

NUTS ∽

A variety of nuts are called for in the recipes here: almonds, macadamias, pecans, pine nuts (pignolis), pistachios, and walnuts. Be sure to always taste nuts for freshness. If they are not to be used for some time, nuts of all kinds are best stored in dry, airtight containers and plastic bags in the freezer. Always allow frozen nuts to come to room temperature before chopping so they do not become soggy or too oily.

If a recipe calls for toasted nuts, do not leave out this important step. Toasting often improves the taste and texture of nuts. However, be sure to watch the nuts carefully while toasting as they burn easily and quickly.

FOLDING ∽

When a recipe calls for "folding in" a specific ingredient, it means to add the ingredient as gently and carefully as possible so that it does not lose its original volume. To accomplish this, stir into the batter a large spoonful of the ingredient. Using a very large rubber spatula, add the rest of the ingredient to the top of the batter. With the spatula, make a movement that goes from the top of the batter through the center to the bottom of the bowl, then quickly pull the spatula up toward you and against the inside wall of the bowl. Spread the batter that has been brought from the bottom of the bowl gently over the top of the mixture with a quick zigzag motion, then rotate the bowl slightly and repeat the entire movement until the ingredient has been completely but carefully incorporated into the batter.

TESTING FOR DONENESS ∾

The very best way to assure that a cake is going to reach the proper doneness, is by making sure your oven is set at the accurate temperature. Oven thermometers are relatively inexpensive and can be purchased at all cooking stores and at most hardware or large department stores. By placing the thermometer on the middle rack in the center of the oven, you'll be able to tell if your oven is set at the temperature the recipe calls for. Even then, though, altitude and humidity and the type of cake pan you use can affect the cooking time. Therefore, it is always best to check the cake slightly before the end of the specified cooking time. Carefully but quickly pull out the oven rack and check first to see if the top of the cake is browning and beginning to pull away from the sides of the pan. Gently touch the top of the cake to see if it springs back lightly.

If so, insert a tester into the center of the cake and see if it comes out clean. (The very best tester is a long metal one that reaches to the bottom of the pan; these testers can be purchased very inexpensively — usually for around a dollar — at most specialty cooking shops.) If the tester comes out clean, the cake is done. If not, return the rack to its original position, gently shut the oven door and test the cake again anywhere from 4 to 10 minutes later, depending on how wet the tester was when drawn from the cake.

Be especially careful when baking *chocolate* pound cakes, which generally cook more quickly than other pound cakes. The tops of chocolate cakes also brown more quickly and more darkly, so it's a good idea to begin testing these cakes 5 or even 10 minutes before the end of the specified cooking time, and then check them again every 4 or 5 minutes until they are properly done.

SPECIAL NOTE: Remember that, unless noted otherwise in the recipe, *all refrigerated ingredients* (such as butter, eggs, milk, cream, sour cream, yogurt, etc.) should be brought to room temperature, but for no more than 1 hour. More than an hour of unrefrigerated time will cause the butter to become too soft and affect the success of the cake, and other items, such as eggs, may spoil.)

Fruit and More . . .

Raspberry Swirl Pound Cake

～ ◆ ～

This recipe makes a cake with a traditional pound cake texture and weight but with an unexpected and delicate flavor. It's also a beautiful and delicious cake, suitable for the most special occasions.

Raspberry swirl:
2 cups fresh raspberries
2 tablespoons red currant jelly
2 tablespoons framboise (raspberry liqueur)
1 tablespoon cornstarch

Cake:
1 cup (2 sticks) butter, room temperature
6 ounces cream cheese, room temperature
2-1/2 cups sugar
6 large eggs, room temperature
3 cups sifted flour
pinch salt
2 teaspoons vanilla extract
3 tablespoons grated or finely minced lemon zest

Preheat oven to 325 degrees.

Butter and flour a 9-inch tube pan.

For the Raspberry Swirl, put raspberries through a food mill or puree in a Cuisinart, being sure to strain out any seeds. Melt jelly in a small saucepan. Add the raspberry puree and warm over low heat.

Dissolve cornstarch in the framboise and add to the saucepan. Bring to a simmer, whisking, until thickened. Remove from heat and cool completely.

For the pound cake, cream together the softened butter and cream cheese until fluffy. Gradually add sugar, beating until lighter and fluffier.

Add eggs, one at a time, beating well after each addition.

Sift the flour with the pinch of salt and then slowly add to the batter, in three additions, being careful not to overbeat. Fold in the vanilla and lemon peel with a spatula.

Place 1/3 of the batter in pan, smoothing it evenly. In a circle, add 1/2 of the raspberry puree, not allowing it to touch the sides of the pan. Add 1/3 of the batter, gently covering the puree. Add the remaining raspberry puree in the same fashion, and finish with the last of the batter.

Bake at 325 degrees for 1 hour and 5-10 minutes, until a tester comes clean. Allow to cool in the pan for 15 minutes before unmolding. Cool completely on a rack.

Fresh Cherry Pound Cake

❧ ✦ ☙

This recipe takes advantage of seasonal fresh cherries; when combined with the richness of ground almonds and the hint of nutmeg, they create a unique and delicious cake.

1 cup (2 sticks) butter, room temperature
1-1/3 cups sugar
4 large eggs, room temperature
2 cups cake flour, sifted with a pinch of salt
3/4 cup slivered almonds, toasted and ground
1-1/2 teaspoons vanilla extract
1/8 teaspoon freshly grated nutmeg
2 full cups unpitted, fresh sweet cherries (after measuring,
the cherries should be pitted and halved)

Preheat oven to 325 degrees.

Butter and flour a 9-inch bundt pan.

Cream butter at medium speed. Slowly add sugar and continue to beat until light, about 4 to 5 minutes.

Add eggs, one at a time, beating well after each addition. With a large rubber spatula, gently fold in the flour. Fold in the almonds, vanilla and nutmeg.

Add 1/3 of the batter to the pan, evenly smoothing it. Arrange a single layer of cherry halves on top of the batter, being careful not to touch the sides of the pan. Repeat with 1/3 more batter, another layer of cherries, and end with the last 1/3 batter, evenly smoothing the top.

Bake for 55-60 minutes, or until a tester comes out clean.

Cool on a rack for 15 minutes then turn out of the bundt pan and cool completely.

SPECIAL NOTE: Remember that, unless noted otherwise in the recipe, *all refrigerated ingredients* (such as butter, eggs, milk, cream, sour cream, yogurt, etc.) should be brought to room temperature, but for no more than 1 hour. More than an hour of unrefrigerated time will cause the butter to become too soft and affect the success of the cake, and other items, such as eggs, may spoil.)

Pineapple-Macadamia Nut Pound Cake

❧ ◆ ☙

To the combination of pineapple and macadamia, a vanilla bean is added to create a cake that is as stunning and exotic as the lands the ingredients come from.

1-1/2 cups crushed pineapple (in heavy syrup)
1 vanilla bean, cut in thirds and split
1 teaspoon vanilla extract
3/4 cup (1-1/2 sticks) butter, room temperature
1 cup light brown sugar
1/2 cup sugar
3 large eggs, room temperature
2-1/4 cups flour
1/2 teaspoon salt
1/2 teaspoon baking powder
2 egg whites (room temperature) plus 1/3 cup sugar
1 full cup macadamia nuts, sliced in chunks

Topping:
2 tablespoons sugar
mixed with 1 teaspoon cinnamon

Preheat the oven to 350 degrees.

Butter and flour a 10-inch tube pan.

Mix the crushed pineapple with the cut vanilla bean, scraping out as many seeds as possible. Add the vanilla extract. Leave the bean in the pineapple while preparing the cake.

In a large mixing bowl cream the butter, slowly adding both the brown sugar and granulated sugar. Add the eggs, one at a time, mixing well after each addition.

Whisk the flour in a bowl with the salt and baking powder to mix. Gently blend the flour into the cake batter.

Beat the egg whites until soft peaks form and slowly add the 1/3 cup sugar. Beat for 2 minutes.

Remove the vanilla bean from the pineapple and then mix the pineapple with the cake batter. Add the macadamia nuts and then gently but thoroughly fold the egg whites into the batter.

Fill the prepared pan with the mixture. Sprinkle with the topping and bake for 55 to 60 minutes or until a cake tester inserted in the center of the cake comes out clean.

Cool the cake on a wire rack for 15 minutes, then turn out onto a rack and cool completely.

Coconut Pound Cake

❧ ✦ ❧

This is an old-fashioned-tasting cake with a white, moist texture, the kind that always seemed to be sitting on the sideboard in my Southern grandmother's dining room.

1-1/4 cups (2-1/2 sticks) butter, room temperature
2-1/2 cups sugar, plus extra 1/2 cup for beating with egg whites
6 large eggs, separated, room temperature
3 cups cake flour
1/2 teaspoon salt
1 cup milk, room temperature
1 teaspoon vanilla extract
1 teaspoon almond extract
2 cups (approximately 8 ounces) fresh frozen coconut,
thawed, and loosely packed

Preheat oven to 325 degrees.

Butter and flour a 10-inch tube pan.

Cream butter until lightened in color, about three minutes. Slowly add the 2-1/2 cups sugar and continue beating at high speed for five minutes. Add the egg yolks, one at a time, beating well after each addition.

Sift the flour with the salt. Alternately add flour and milk to the batter. Add the extracts and mix the coconut well into the batter.

Beat the egg whites until foamy; slowly add the 1/2 cup sugar and beat until the whites are stiff. Gently but thoroughly fold into the batter.

Pour into the prepared tube pan and bake for 1 hour and 50 minutes at 325 degrees.

Cool in the pan on a rack for 15 minutes, then turn out cake on a wire rack and cool completely before slicing. Store this cake in the refrigerator. When serving, slice and bring to room temperature.

Glazed Banana Pound Cake

～ ◆ ～

Don't let the name of this cake mislead you into thinking it is similar to a banana nut bread. Instead, it's a spicy pound cake with a light, appealing texture.

1 cup (2 sticks) butter, room temperature
2-3/4 cups sugar, plus an additional 1/4 cup sugar
6 large eggs, separated, room temperature
1 cup sour cream, room temperature
2 large, very ripe bananas, mashed to make 1 full cup
1-1/2 teaspoons vanilla extract
3 cups cake flour
1/2 teaspoon baking soda
1/4 teaspoon salt
1/2 teaspoon freshly grated nutmeg
1/2 teaspoon allspice
1/4 teaspoon cloves
1/2 teaspoon ginger

Glaze:
2 cups confectioners' sugar, sifted
2-3 tablespoons water

Preheat oven to 325 degrees.

Butter and flour a 10-1/2-inch decorative tube or bundt pan.

Cream the softened butter well, slowly adding the 2-3/4 cups sugar. Beat the mixture for about 5 minutes. Add the egg yolks and beat well.

Mix together the sour cream, mashed bananas, and vanilla extract. Add the sour cream mixture to the batter.

In a bowl, whisk together the flour, baking soda, salt, and spices. Gently fold the flour into the cake batter.

With clean, dry beaters, beat the egg whites until they hold soft peaks. Add the 1/4 cup sugar to the egg whites and continue beating until firm. Fold the egg whites into the batter, being careful not to overmix.

Pour the cake batter into the prepared pan and bake at 325 degrees for 1 hour and 15-20 minutes, checking with a tester for doneness.

Let the cake cool in the pan on a wire rack for 15 minutes. Unmold on a rack and cool completely.

To glaze the cake:

Combine the confectioners' sugar and the water, mixing well. Place the cooled cake on a wire rack over a sheet of waxed paper. Slowly drizzle the glaze over the cake, covering completely.

Summer Blueberry Pound Cake

❦ ◆ ❧

This is a particularly good pound cake full of fresh blueberries with a refreshing hint of lemon and orange.

1 cup (2 sticks) butter, room temperature
2 cups sugar
4 large eggs, separated, room temperature
3 cups flour
2 teaspoons baking powder
1/2 teaspoon salt
1/2 cup milk, room temperature
1 teaspoon orange extract
1 tablespoon finely grated orange zest (about 3 oranges)
2 teaspoons finely grated lemon zest (2 large lemons)
2 cups fresh blueberries, rinsed and dried well,
then tossed in 1 tablespoon flour

Preheat oven to 350 degrees.

Butter and flour a 9-1/2-inch bundt pan.

Cream the softened butter for 2 minutes, then add the sugar and cream on high speed for 5 minutes more. Add the egg yolks, one at a time, beating well after each addition.

Sift the flour with the baking powder and salt.

Add half the flour to the mixture, blending well, then add the 1/2 cup milk. Lastly, add the remaining flour.

Gently add the orange extract, orange zest and lemon zest. Fold in the blueberries.

Beat the egg whites until stiff and gently fold into the cake batter.

Bake in a 350-degree oven for 55-60 minutes, or until the cake tests done.

Cool on a cake rack for 15 minutes. Unmold and cool completely.

Candied Orange Pound Cake

꿍 ♦ 꿍

This is one of my all-time favorites, with its cool, clean citrus flavor. And, since it is a smaller, loaf cake, it is perfect for gift-giving or for packing in the picnic basket.

3/4 cup (1-1/2 sticks) butter, room temperature
1-1/2 cups sugar
4 large eggs, room temperature
1-1/2 cups flour
3/4 teaspoon orange extract
2 tablespoons orange juice
3/4 cup chopped candied orange rind *

Preheat oven to 350 degrees.

Butter and flour a 9x 5x 3-inch loaf pan.

Cream the butter until lightened in color. Slowly add the sugar and continue beating about 5 minutes. Add eggs, one at a time, mixing well after each addition. Gradually add the flour, mixing well.

Fold in the orange extract, orange juice, and candied orange rind. Turn the batter into the loaf pan and bake for 50 to 60 minutes, or until a tester comes out clean.

Allow the cake to cool in pan on wire rack for about 10 minutes, then turn out on rack and let the cake cool completely.

* Candied orange rind can be found at Williams Sonoma cook stores and local groceries or farmers' markets. Or, you can make your own using the following recipe.

Candied Orange Rind:
2 cups orange peel, chopped into small squares
1-1/2 cups cold water
1/2 cup water
1 cup sugar

Place the chopped orange peel in a heavy saucepan along with the 1-1/2 cups cold water. Slowly bring to a boil and simmer for 10 to 12 minutes. Drain. Repeat the simmering process 4 or 5 more times, draining well each time.

Meanwhile, combine the 1/2 cup water and 1 cup of sugar in a saucepan. Bring to a boil. Add the drained orange peel and boil until all the syrup is absorbed and the peel is transparent. Check often to make sure the chopped orange peel doesn't stick or scorch. Dry on a wire rack or wire mesh. The drying process will take a full day in dry weather and longer if it's humid. Store the Candied Orange Rind in airtight containers until ready to use.

Apple Ginger Pound Cake
with Custard Sauce

❧ ◆ ❧

It took countless throw-aways to come up with a great apple pound cake. But this cake, especially when paired with the ginger-flavored custard sauce, was well worth all the testing.

1 cup (2 sticks) butter, room temperature
1-3/4 cups sugar
5 large eggs, room temperature
2 cups flour
1/4 teaspoon salt
1 teaspoon dried ginger
1/4 teaspoon cinnamon
1/4 teaspoon freshly grated nutmeg
1/4 cup cream, room temperature
1 teaspoon finely grated lemon zest
1 cup peeled and finely chopped Granny Smith apples,
tossed in 2 teaspoons fresh lemon juice

Custard Sauce:
1-3/4 cups Half and Half
5 large egg yolks

1/2 cup sugar
1 teaspoon vanilla extract
1/2 teaspoon dried ginger
1 teaspoon fresh lemon juice

Preheat oven to 350 degrees.

Butter and flour a 9 x 5 x 3-inch loaf pan.

Cream the butter for 3 minutes, until lightened in color. Add the sugar and beat on high speed for 5 minutes. Add the eggs, one at a time, beating well after each addition.

Sift the flour with the salt, ginger, cinnamon, and nutmeg. Gradually add the flour to the batter, blending well.

Add the 1/4 cup cream and blend well.

Mix in the lemon zest. Fold in the chopped apples and lemon juice.

Spoon batter into the loaf pan and bake at 350 degrees for about 1 hour, or until it tests done.

Cool in the pan about 10 minutes, then turn out on a cake rack and cool completely.

For the Custard Sauce:

Bring the Half and Half to a simmer and remove from heat. Beat the egg yolks and sugar in a medium saucepan until they reach a nice pale yellow.

Slowly add the warm Half and Half to the egg yolks,

whisking constantly over low heat until the sauce coats a spoon, being especially careful not to curdle the yolks.

Transfer the ingredients to a glass bowl. Whisk in the vanilla extract and dried ginger and lemon juice. Allow to cool before refrigerating.

The Custard Sauce makes a nice addition to the Apple Ginger Pound Cake when spooned on top of each slice or to the side of the dessert place. The sauce can be refrigerated for 2 days.

SPECIAL NOTE: Remember that, unless noted otherwise in the recipe, *all refrigerated ingredients* (such as butter, eggs, milk, cream, sour cream, yogurt, etc.) should be brought to room temperature, but for no more than 1 hour. More than an hour of unrefrigerated time will cause the butter to become too soft and affect the success of the cake, and other items, such as eggs, may spoil.)

Apricot, Cream Cheese, & Walnut Pound Cake

❧ ◆ ❧

This cake proves that it's hard to go wrong with a fresh fruit, nuts, and cream cheese especially when the fruit is as distinctive as apricots. The result is a cake full of flavor and texture that is a perfect accompaniment to coffee or tea.

1 cup (2 sticks) butter, room temperature
3 ounces cream cheese, room temperature
2 cups sugar
5 large eggs, room temperature
2-1/2 cups flour
1 teaspoon baking powder
1/2 teaspoon baking soda
1-1/2 teaspoons finely grated orange zest
3/4 teaspoon orange extract
1 teaspoon freshly grated nutmeg
1 cup chopped walnuts
1-1/2 cups diced fresh apricots (approximately
4-5 medium apricots, unpeeled)

Preheat oven to 325 degrees.
Butter and flour a 10-inch tube pan.

Cream together butter and cream cheese for about 5 minutes. Slowly add the sugar to the creamed mixture, beating until lighter in texture.

Add the eggs to the batter, one at a time, beating well after each addition.

In a bowl, whisk together the flour, baking powder, and soda. Gently but thoroughly blend the dry ingredients into the batter. Beat for 1 minute to incorporate the flour.

Add the orange zest, orange extract and nutmeg.

Fold in the walnuts and diced apricots.

Evenly spread the batter into the prepared pan and bake in a 325-degree oven for about 1 hour and 10-15 minutes, or until a tester comes out clean.

Cool in the pan on a wire rack for about 10 minutes. Turn the cake out onto a wire rack and allow to cool completely before slicing.

Grandmother Bibb's Prune Pound Cake
with Walnut Icing

❧ ✦ ❧

This recipe has been passed from mother to daughter to grand-daughter and is a family favorite. Don't be put off by the prunes; they make a moist, rich, and absolutely delicious cake.

3/4 cup (1-1/2 sticks) butter, room temperature
2 cups sugar
3 large eggs, room temperature
2 cups flour
1 teaspoon baking soda
1 teaspoon salt
1 teaspoon cinnamon
1 teaspoon cloves
1 teaspoon freshly grated nutmeg
1 cup buttermilk, room temperature
1 teaspoon vanilla extract
1 cup cooked mashed prunes

Walnut Icing:
1/4 cup butter
1 cup sugar

1/2 teaspoon baking soda
1/2 cup buttermilk
2 teaspoons white Karo syrup
1 full cup finely chopped walnuts
1/2 teaspoon vanilla extract

Preheat oven to 300 degrees.

Butter and flour a 9-inch bundt pan.

Cream the softened butter until it lightens in color. Add the sugar and continue to beat for 3 minutes. Beat in the eggs, one at a time, and mix well.

In a bowl, whisk together the flour, soda, salt, and spices. Alternately add the flour and buttermilk to the batter in the following manner: 1/3 flour; 1/2 buttermilk; 1/3 flour; 1/2 buttermilk; then the remaining 1/3 flour.

Fold in the vanilla and prunes. Transfer to the prepared bundt pan and bake in a 300-degree oven 55-60 minutes.

As soon as the cake is in the oven, combine the icing ingredients in a saucepan, except the vanilla, and allow to simmer about 45 minutes to 1 hour, until it becomes darker in color and thicker. Let the icing cool off the heat as the finished cake cools in the bundt pan on a rack (about 15 minutes). Turn the cake out onto a rack placed on a sheet of waxed paper and slowly spoon the icing onto the warm cake. Allow the cake to cool completely before slicing.

Cranberry Walnut Pound Cake

❦ ◆ ❦

Since this recipe calls for dried cranberries, it can be made and enjoyed any time of the year. But once baked during the holidays, expect it to become a Christmas tradition.

1 cup (2 sticks) butter, room temperature
2-1/2 cups sugar
6 large eggs, room temperature
2/3 cup jellied cranberry sauce, whisked until smooth
3 cups flour
1/4 teaspoon salt
1 teaspoon baking soda
1/2 cup buttermilk, room temperature
1 tablespoon finely grated orange zest (about 3 oranges)
1/2 teaspoon orange extract
3/4 cup chopped walnuts
*1 cup plus an additional 1/2 cup dried cranberries (found
in specialty cook shops or local farmers' markets)*

Preheat oven to 325 degrees.
Butter and flour a 10-inch tube pan.
Cream the butter for 2 minutes, until lightened in color.

Gradually add the sugar and beat on high speed for 5 minutes. Add the eggs, one at a time, beating well after each addition. Mix the cranberry sauce well into the batter.

Sift together the flour, salt and soda. Add 1/2 of the flour to the batter, blending well, then add the buttermilk. Add the remaining flour.

Blend the zest and orange extract well into batter. Fold in the chopped walnuts and 1 cup cranberries. Pour the batter into the prepared pan. Sprinkle the remaining 1/2 cup cranberries on top of the cake and lightly push into the batter with a rubber spatula.

Bake in the tube pan in a 325-degree oven for about 1 hour and 5 to 10 minutes, or until the cake tests done.

Cool in the pan for 15 minutes, then turn out onto a rack and cool completely.

The
Chocolate
Experience

Buttermilk Chocolate Pound Cake

꧁ ✦ ꧂

After testing countless plain chocolate pound cakes, this was the absolute favorite, the one that tasted the most like the simple chocolate pound cakes of my childhood. It's also one of those cakes that is even better on the second or third day. (Remember that chocolate cakes tend to bake more quickly than other cakes, so be particularly careful not to overcook it.)

sifted cocoa, for preparing the baking pan
2 cups (4 sticks) butter, room temperature
3 cups sugar
6 large eggs, room temperature
3-1/4 cups flour
1/4 teaspoon salt
1/2 teaspoon baking soda
3/4 cup cocoa
3/4 cup buttermilk, room temperature
1-1/2 teaspoon vanilla

Preheat oven to 350 degrees.

Butter a 9-1/2-inch tube pan. Dust with sifted cocoa (instead of flour).

Cream the butter with an electric mixer. Add the sugar gradually and continue to beat for 5 minutes.

Add the eggs, one at a time, mixing well after each one.

In a separate bowl, using a wire whisk or fork, mix together the flour, salt, baking soda, and cocoa. Alternately add the dry ingredients and the buttermilk and vanilla to the batter, ending with the flour.

Pour into the prepared tube pan and bake at 350 degrees for approximately 1 hour and 10 to 15 minutes, being extra careful not to overcook.

Let the finished cake cool in the pan for 10 minutes. Then turn the cake out on a wire rack and let it cool completely.

Chocolate Walnut Pound Cake

❧ ✦ ❧

This cake has a double dose of chocolate and stays fresh and moist for several days.

sifted cocoa, for preparing the baking pan
1 cup (2 sticks) butter, room temperature
1-1/3 cups sugar
3 large eggs, room temperature
1-2/3 cups flour
1/3 cup cocoa
1/2 teaspoon baking soda
1/4 teaspoon salt
1 cup vanilla yogurt, room temperature
1 teaspoon vanilla extract
2/3 cup coarsely chopped walnuts
2 3-ounce bars bittersweet chocolate, chopped

Preheat oven to 325 degrees.

Butter a 9 x 5 x 3-inch loaf pan. Dust with sifted cocoa (instead of flour).

Cream the butter with an electric mixer. Add the sugar gradually and continue to beat for 5 minutes.

Add the eggs, one at a time, mixing well after each one.

In a separate bowl, sift together the flour, cocoa, soda, and salt. Alternately add the dry ingredients and the vanilla yogurt to the batter, ending with the flour. Mix in the vanilla extract, nuts, and chopped chocolate.

Pour into the prepared loaf pan and bake at 325 degrees for approximately 1 hour and 10 to 15 minutes, being extra careful not to overcook.

Let the finished cake cool in the pan for 10 minutes. Then turn the cake out on a wire rack and let it cool completely.

Chocolate Chip Cookie Pound Cake

꩜ ♦ ꩜

This cake has all the ingredients of a true chocolate chip cook-ie and will become just as loved, especially in households with children.

1-1/2 cups chocolate chips
1 cup (2 sticks) butter, room temperature
1 cup sugar
1-1/2 cups firmed packed light brown sugar
5 large eggs, room temperature
3 cups flour
1 cup sour cream, room temperature
1 tablespoon vanilla extract
1 teaspoon baking powder
1/2 teaspoon baking soda
1/2 teaspoon salt
1 cup chopped pecans

Preheat the oven to 325 degrees.

Butter and flour a 10-inch tube pan.

Place chocolate chips in a food processor, pulsing just until the chips are chopped finely but not so long that they become too powdery. Set aside.

Beat the butter until light. Add the sugars, a little at a time, and cream very well — until the mixture is light and fluffy.

Beat in the eggs, one at a time, beating slightly after each addition.

Mix in 1/2 of the flour.

Mix together the sour cream and vanilla and add to the batter, mixing well. Combine the baking powder, soda and salt with remaining flour and add to the batter. Mix well.

Add the chopped chocolate chips and the cup of pecans, incorporating well with the rest of the batter but being careful not to overbeat at this point.

Bake at 325 degrees for 55 to 60 minutes or until a cake tester or knife inserted in the center of the cake comes out clean.

Let the cake cool in the pan for 15 to 20 minutes before turning out on a cake rack. Cool completely before slicing.

Oreo Pound Cake

❧ ◆ ❧

Although the name of this cake makes it a real hit with school-aged children, it's also loved by grown-ups as well.

2 cups crushed Oreo cookies (about 18 to 20 cookies)
1-1/2 cups (3 sticks) butter, room temperature
2 cups sugar
5 large eggs, room temperature
3 cups flour
1 teaspoon baking powder
1 cup cream, room temperature
1 tablespoon vanilla extract

Preheat oven to 325 degrees.

Butter and flour a 10-inch tube pan.

Crush between two pieces of waxed paper enough Oreos (approximately 18 to 20 cookies) to measure 2 cups after crushing. Put aside for later use.

Cream together the softened butter and the sugar until light and smooth. Add eggs, one at a time, beating after each addition.

Combine the flour and baking powder. Add 1/2 of the flour

mixture to the batter and beat well.

Add the cream and vanilla to batter and mix. Add the remaining 1/2 flour and mix well.

Add the crushed Oreos and mix just until incorporated well, being careful not to over-mix.

Pour the batter into prepared tube pan.

Bake for 1 hour and 10-15 minutes or until the cake pulls away from the sides of the pan and a tester inserted in the center of the cake comes out clean.

Let the cake cool in the pan on a wire rack for 10-15 minutes. Turn the cake out on a rack and let cool completely.

Mocha Pound Cake
with Coffee Creme Anglaise

❦ ✦ ❧

The coffee and cocoa compliment one another nicely in this recipe and make a moist, delicious pound cake that is liked by all, especially when served with the Coffee Creme Anglaise.

1 cup (2 sticks) butter, room temperature
1/2 cup Crisco
3-1/4 cups sugar
5 large eggs, room temperature
3 cups flour
4 tablespoons cocoa
1/2 teaspoon baking powder
1/2 teaspoon baking soda
1 cup coffee yogurt, room temperature
1/2 cup strong coffee
1 tablespoon vanilla extract

Preheat the oven to 325 degrees.

Butter and flour a 10-inch tube pan.

Cream together the butter and Crisco, beating well. Add the sugar and beat until fluffy. Add the eggs one at a time.

Whisk together the flour, cocoa, baking powder, and baking soda. Alternately add the dry ingredients and the coffee yogurt to the batter, ending with the flour mixture. Combine the coffee and vanilla extract and carefully fold into the batter.

Bake at 325 degrees for one hour and 15 to 20 minutes or until a cake tester inserted in the center of the cake comes out clean.

Cool in the pan on a rack for 15 minutes, then turn out onto a rack and cool completely. Serve with the optional Coffee Creme Anglaise.

For the Coffee Creme Anglaise:

2 cups milk

1 tablespoon instant coffee

5 large egg yolks

2 teaspoons cornstarch

1/2 cup sugar

1-1/2 teaspoons vanilla extract

2 tablespoons strong coffee

Warm the milk and coffee until hot, but don't let the mixture simmer.

In a medium saucepan, combine the egg yolks, cornstarch and sugar. Whisk over low heat until mixture thickens. Slowly add the warm milk and instant coffee, stirring until the mixture coats the back of a spoon.

Stir in the vanilla extract and strong coffee. Allow the custard to cool. Place a piece of plastic wrap directly on the custard and then refrigerate. This recipe can be made 2 to 3 days ahead of time.

SPECIAL NOTE: Remember that, unless noted otherwise in the recipe, *all refrigerated ingredients* (such as butter, eggs, milk, cream, sour cream, yogurt, etc.) should be brought to room temperature, but for no more than 1 hour. More than an hour of unrefrigerated time will cause the butter to become too soft and affect the success of the cake, and other items, such as eggs, may spoil.)

Chocolate Truffle Pound Cake

❧ ◆ ❧

This is the ultimate chocolate pound cake, the one rich
enough and elegant enough to please all chocolate lovers
and to serve at the most special occasions.

1 cup (2 sticks) butter, room temperature
3 cups light brown sugar
6 large eggs, room temperature
2-1/2 cups flour
1 teaspoon baking soda
1/2 teaspoon salt
1/2 cup cocoa
1 cup buttermilk, room temperature
6 ounces bittersweet chocolate, melted
1 tablespoon vanilla extract

Chocolate Truffle Icing:
3/4 cup butter, softened
1 box confectioners' sugar
1/2 cup plus 1 tablespoon cocoa
5-6 tablespoons buttermilk
cocoa, for dusting
1/2 cup chopped toasted almonds

Preheat oven to 325 degrees.

Butter and flour a 10-inch tube pan.

Cream the butter until lightened in color. Add the brown sugar gradually until well combined. Continue to beat for about 5 minutes.

Add the eggs, one at a time, mixing well after each addition.

In a bowl whisk together the flour, soda, salt, and cocoa. Add 1/3 of the dry ingredients to the batter, mix well, and then add 1/2 cup of the buttermilk. Add the next 1/3 flour, the remaining buttermilk, and finally the last 1/3 flour. Beat about 1 minute to mix well.

Gently fold in the melted chocolate and vanilla. Pour the batter into prepared pan and smooth the top.

Bake at 325 degrees for 1 hour and 15 to 20 minutes or until a cake tester comes out clean. (Be careful not to overbake, checking the cake after 70 minutes.)

Let the cake rest in the pan for 15 to 20 minutes; turn out, then let cool completely before icing.

For the *Chocolate Truffle Icing*, combine well all ingredients until light and fluffy, adding additional buttermilk if necessary to make spreadable. Ice the cooled cake. Dust the top with cocoa (shaking through a strainer or sifter), and sprinkle chopped almonds on top.

From the
Old-Fashioned
Pantry

Susan's Orange Pound Cake

❧ ◆ ❧

This makes a light, airy cake that is perfect for slicing and toasting at tea time, which is the way many of those who were brought up on it in the Bibb family like it best. It is different from most other pound cake recipes because the pan is placed in a COLD oven rather than a preheated one.

1-1/2 cups (3 sticks) butter, room temperature
2 cups sugar
6 large eggs, room temperature
3 cups sifted flour
2 tablespoons orange extract (1 fluid ounce jar)

Butter and flour a 10-inch tube pan.

Cream together butter and sugar.

Add eggs, one at a time, beating well after each addition.

Add flour gradually (turn mixer setting to "blend"). Add orange extract.

Pour batter into the prepared pan. Place cake into a **COLD** oven. Set temperature at 325 degrees and bake for one hour and 15 minutes.

The recipe also may be halved and cooked in a loaf pan,

or the batter may be divided and put into two loaf pans; if so, check the cakes after 40 minutes of cooking time.

Note: It is best to keep this cake at room temperature after baking; refrigeration alters the texture, making the cake denser and heavier.

French Vanilla Pound Cake

❧ ✦ ☙

This cake, like Susan's Orange Pound Cake, is placed in a cold oven, and it has an intense vanilla taste because of the real vanilla bean.

1 vanilla bean, cut into thirds
1 cup cream, room temperature
1-1/4 cups (2-1/2 sticks) butter, room temperature
2-1/2 cups sugar
6 large eggs, room temperature
3 cups cake flour
1 teaspoon baking powder
1 tablespoon vanilla extract
1 teaspoon lemon extract

Butter and flour a large (10-1/2-inch) decorative bundt pan. With a small knife split in half the vanilla bean pieces. Place the vanilla bean and cream in a small saucepan. Warm the mixture just to a simmer, making sure it doesn't come to a boil. Remove from the heat and allow the mixture to steep while preparing the cake.

Cream the butter on high speed and then slowly add the

sugar; continue beating for about 5 minutes. Add the eggs, one at a time, mixing well after each addition.

Sift the cake flour with the baking powder, and set aside.

Remove the vanilla bean pieces from the cream; using a small knife, thoroughly scrape the insides of the pieces into the cream. Discard the pieces.

Alternately add the flour and cream to the batter, beginning and ending with the flour. Beat in the extracts and then pour the batter into the prepared pan.

Place in a COLD oven and bake at 325 degrees for 65 minutes, or until a tester comes out clean.

Allow the cake to cool in the pan on a wire rack for about 15 minutes, then turn out and cool completely.

Liza's Pound Cake

❧ ◆ ❧

This traditional and very large pound cake is a favorite family recipe that was given to Liza by her Aunt Maria from Montgomery.

Pam, or similar non-stick cooking spray
8 large eggs, room temperature
3 cups sugar
1 cup (2 sticks) butter, room temperature
1/2 teaspoon baking soda
1/4 teaspoon salt
1 full teaspoon vanilla extract
1 full teaspoon almond extract
3 cups flour
1 cup sour cream, room temperature

Preheat oven to 350 degrees.

Spray a heavy, dark interior 10-inch bundt pan with Pam. (This kind of pan will ensure a dark, wonderful crust.)

Place the first seven ingredients in a mixer and beat 10 minutes on high speed.

Sift the flour and then add to the batter, 1 cup at a time,

with speed on medium. Add the sour cream.

Bake the cake at 350 degrees for about 20 to 30 minutes; the top of the cake will be brown. Turn down the oven temperature to 300 degrees and continue baking about 45 minutes. (The total cooking time will be about 1 hour and 15 minutes, or until the cake tests done.)

Cool in pan on cake rack about 15 minutes, then turn out on a rack and cool completely.

Note: This recipe can be halved and will fill 1 loaf pan, or the whole recipe will make 2 loaf cakes. If you use loaf pans instead of the bundt pan, cook for approximately 45 minutes, or until the cake tests done.

Lemon Cream Cheese Pound Cake

❧ ◆ ❧

This is a very pretty dessert with the dusting of confectioners' sugar making a lacy pattern on top of the cake. For those with a sweeter tooth, there is an optional lemon glaze that can be used instead. The cake is baked in a springform pan instead of the usual tube, bundt, or loaf pan.

1 tablespoon finely grated lemon zest, about 3 medium lemons
1 cup (2 sticks) butter, room temperature
8 ounces cream cheese, room temperature
2 cups sugar
6 large eggs, room temperature
2 cups self-rising flour
2 teaspoons lemon extract
confectioners' sugar, for dusting
paper doily

Preheat oven to 325 degrees.

Butter and flour the sides of a 9-inch springform pan. Cut a circle of wax paper to fit inside the bottom of the pan and butter and flour the wax paper.

Carefully grate the lemon zest, using only the yellow outer rind (the white, pithy part of the rind can be bitter and alter the taste). It may take as many as three lemons, depending on their size, to get one full tablespoon of zest.

Cream together the softened butter and cream cheese. Add sugar, gradually, and beat well. Add eggs, one at a time, beating after each one.

Add flour, lemon extract, and lemon zest. Mix well.

Pour into the springform pan. Bake for 45 to 50 minutes at 325 degrees, being careful not to overcook, which makes the cake too dry. Cake is done when tester comes out clean.

When the cake has fully cooled, place a paper doily (or a clean piece of paper that has been cut in an intricate snowflake design) over the cake and sift confectioners' sugar over it. The cake stands alone as is but if you prefer a sweeter cake, you can replace the dusting of confectioners' sugar with the following lemon glaze.

Lemon Glaze: (optional)
1 cup confectioners' sugar
3 tablespoons milk
1 teaspoon lemon extract
1 teaspoon finely grated lemon zest

Beat together the confectioners' sugar and milk until the consistency is smooth and creamy. Add extract and lemon rind. Spread the glaze over lemon cream cheese pound cake while the cake is still warm.

Almond Pound Cake

❧ ◆ ☙

For those who like a basic, old-fashioned pound cake, this is an excellent one—with just a hint of almond.

2 cups (4 sticks) butter, room temperature
3 cups sugar
6 large eggs, room temperature
1 cup milk, room temperature
1 tablespoon vanilla extract
1 tablespoon almond extract
4 cups flour

Preheat oven to 325 degrees.

Butter and flour a 10-inch tube pan.

Cream together the softened butter and the sugar on high speed of an electric mixture for several minutes. Add eggs, one at a time, and beat well. Combine the milk with the extracts. Alternately add flour and liquid to the batter. Mix well.

Pour into a 10-inch tube pan and bake at 325 degrees for 1-1/2 hours to 1 hour and 50 minutes or until a tester comes out clean.

Cool the cake in the pan on a rack for 15 minutes, then turn the cake out onto a rack and cool completely.

Half-a-Pound Cake

❧ ◆ ❧

This is a smaller, simple cake that is great for toasting and serving with jam or ice cream. It would also be nice paired with the Coffee Creme Anglaise (page 40).

1 cup (2 sticks) butter, room temperature
1-2/3 cups sugar
5 large eggs, room temperature
2 cups cake flour
1-1/2 teaspoons vanilla extract

Preheat oven to 350 degrees.

Butter and flour a 9-inch bundt pan.

Cream the butter; gradually add the sugar and beat well. Add eggs, one at a time, mixing well after each addition. Add the flour gradually, mixing well. Add the vanilla extract, being careful not to overmix at this point.

Pour into the prepared bundt pan, and smooth the top of the batter. Bake at 350 degrees for 45 to 50 minutes.

Cool in the pan on a wire rack for 15 minutes, then turn out cake on a rack and cool completely.

13 Colonies Pound Cake

❧ ✦ ❧

This is an example of a traditional pound cake in which the recipe called for a pound of butter, a pound of sugar, and a pound of flour. It contains only basic ingredients, that would have been part of a typical colonist's larder, and standard spices such as cinnamon, ginger, and nutmeg. This makes a large cake full of old-fashioned flavor.

1 pound butter (4 sticks), room temperature
1 pound sugar (2-1/4 cups)
1 pound eggs (8 large eggs), room temperature
1 pound flour (3-1/3 cups)
1/4 teaspoon salt
1 tablespoon cinnamon
1 teaspoon freshly grated nutmeg
1 teaspoon ginger
1/2 teaspoon ground cloves
2 teaspoons vanilla extract

Preheat oven to 350 degrees.
Butter and flour a 10-inch tube pan.
Cream together the butter and sugar, beating well. Add eggs

one at a time, mixing well after each one.

Add 1/3 of the flour at a time, beating well after each addition. Add the salt, cinnamon, nutmeg, ginger, cloves, and vanilla, incorporating completely.

Pour into the prepared tube pan and bake at 350 degrees for 1 hour and 20 to 25 minutes, or until a tester comes out clean.

Let the cake rest in the pan for 10 minutes, then turn out onto a wire rack and allow to cool completely.

SPECIAL NOTE: Remember that, unless noted otherwise in the recipe, *all refrigerated ingredients* (such as butter, eggs, milk, cream, sour cream, yogurt, etc.) should be brought to room temperature, but for no more than 1 hour. More than an hour of unrefrigerated time will cause the butter to become too soft and affect the success of the cake, and other items, such as eggs, may spoil.)

Outrageously
Inspired

Pistachio Pound Cake

❦ ◆ ❧

This cake was created especially for pictachio lovers but, with its unique taste and texture, it has become with a hit with everyone who tries it.

1 cup (2 sticks) butter, room temperature

2-1/2 cups sugar

6 large eggs, room temperature

3 cups flour

1/2 teaspoon salt

1/2 cup cream, room temperature

3/4 teaspoon almond extract

2 teaspoons vanilla extract

1-1/2 teaspoons lemon extract

1-1/2 cups chopped pistachios

Preheat oven to 325 degrees.

Butter and flour a 10-inch tube pan.

Cream butter on high speed for 2-3 minutes. Slowly add sugar and continue beating for 5 minutes. Add eggs, one at a time, mixing well after each addition.

Sift together the flour and salt. Add 1/2 the flour to the batter.

Mix in the cream and then the remaining flour.

Beat in the extracts. Fold in the chopped pistachios.

Pour batter into the prepared pan and bake at 325 degrees for 1 hour and 10-12 minutes or until a tester comes out clean.

Let the cake sit in the pan on a wire rack for about 15 minutes, then turn out onto a rack to cool completely.

Note: This cake does not freeze well, but it will keep in the refrigerator for about 5 days.

Sweet Potato Pound Cake

❦ ✦ ❦

This is a spicy, aromatic cake that is especially good when served with the Spiced Whipped Cream. It's delicious any time of the year but seems particularly nice in the fall or winter. It's dedicated to the memory of Deleen Woodall and Ella Jordan, who made some of the best sweet potato pies in the world.

1 cup (2 sticks) butter, room temperature

2 cups sugar

4 large eggs, room temperature

2 cups cooked and mashed sweet potatoes

2-1/2 cups flour

1/4 teaspoon salt

1 teaspoon baking powder

1 teaspoon baking soda

1/2 teaspoon freshly grated nutmeg

1 teaspoon cinnamon

1/8 teaspoon ground cloves

1/4 cup orange juice

1 teaspoon finely grated lemon zest

Spiced Whipped Cream:
2 cups cream
1/4 cup sugar, or to desired sweetness
1/4 teaspoon nutmeg
1/2 teaspoon cinnamon

Preheat oven to 325 degrees.

Butter and flour a 9-1/2-inch bundt pan.

Cream at high speed the 1 cup butter and then on medium speed mix in sugar. Continue to beat until lighter in color and texture. Add eggs, one at a time, beating well after each addition. Then mix in the mashed sweet potatoes thoroughly.

Whisk the flour, salt, baking powder, baking soda, and spices together in a bowl. Gently fold in the flour, just until mixed. Next, fold in the orange juice and lemon zest.

Pour into prepared bundt pan. Bake at 325 degrees for 55 to 60 minutes. Cool in pan on rack for 10 to 15 minutes, then turn out and let cool completely.

Serve a dollop of the Spiced Whipped Cream with each slice of cake.

To make the **Spiced Whipped Cream**, whip cold cream with chilled beaters until soft peaks start to form, then add the sugar and spices and whip until desired consistency. (This recipe also would go nicely with Bourbon Pecan Pound Cake or Cranberry Walnut Pound Cake.)

Southern Chess Pound Cake

❦ ◆ ❦

This cake is dedicated to our beloved Jack Kidd, who loved life and a good chess pie.

1 cup (2 sticks) butter, room temperature
1/2 cup Crisco
3 cups sugar
5 large eggs, room temperature
2-1/4 cups flour
3/4 cup yellow cornmeal
1 teaspoon baking powder
1/4 teaspoon salt
1/2 teaspoon baking soda
1 cup buttermilk, room temperature
1 tablespoon vanilla extract
2 tablespoons lemon juice

Preheat oven to 300 degrees.

Butter and flour a 10-inch tube pan.

Cream the softened butter and Crisco until lightened in color, about 3 minutes. Slowly add the sugar and then beat at high speed for 5 minutes. Add the eggs, one at a time, beating well after each addition.

Sift together the flour, cornmeal, baking powder, salt and baking soda. Add 1/3 of the flour to batter, gently blending in, then add 1/2 cup buttermilk. Repeat with the remaining flour mixture and buttermilk, ending with the flour.

Mix in the vanilla and lemon juice.

Bake in a 300-degree oven about 1 hour and 15 minutes, or until the cake tests done. Cool in the pan for 15 minutes, then turn out on a cake rack and cool completely.

Note: This cake will look somewhat fallen and crusty, much like a true chess pie, and its taste will be wonderful.

SPECIAL NOTE: Remember that, unless noted otherwise in the recipe, *all refrigerated ingredients* (such as butter, eggs, milk, cream, sour cream, yogurt, etc.) should be brought to room temperature, but for no more than 1 hour. More than an hour of unrefrigerated time will cause the butter to become too soft and affect the success of the cake, and other items, such as eggs, may spoil.)

Toasted Pecan & Brown Sugar Pound Cake
with Caramel Sauce

❧ ◆ ❧

This is a really wonderful cake that has a surprisingly light texture. It is a perfect make-ahead dessert that is dressy enough to serve at a large dinner party.

1/2 cup (1 stick) butter, room temperature
2-1/2 cups light brown sugar
2 tablespoons lemon juice
6 large eggs, room temperature
2-3/4 cups cake flour
1/2 teaspoon baking soda
1/2 teaspoon salt
1 cup sour cream, room temperature
1 tablespoon vanilla extract
*2 full cups pecan halves, toasted at 325 degrees for 10
minutes, then coarsely chopped*

Caramel Sauce:
1-1/2 cups sugar
3/4 cup water
3/4 cup cream

Preheat oven to 325 degrees.

Butter and flour a 10-inch tube pan.

Cream the butter and sugar on high speed for 5 minutes, then add the lemon juice and beat two more minutes.

Add the eggs, one at a time, mixing well after each addition.

Sift the flour with the soda and salt. Combine the cream and vanilla extract.

Add 1/2 of the flour to the batter, blending well, then add all of the sour cream, again mixing well. Blend in the remaining flour.

Fold in the chopped toasted pecans.

Transfer the batter to the tube pan and bake approximately 60 to 70 minutes, or until a cake tester inserted in the center of the cake comes out clean. Let cool completely.

For serving, give each person a generous slice of cake and pass the bowl of chilled Caramel Sauce.

For the **Caramel Sauce**, place the sugar and water in a small heavy saucepan. Over medium-high heat stir to dissolve the sugar. After the crystals have dissolved, let the syrup boil until it turns a golden brown color. Be careful not to let it burn or turn too dark.

Remove saucepan from heat and gradually add the cream. Whisk until smooth and return to low heat and cook until it thickens slightly, about 5 minutes. Let the sauce cool, then refrigerate.

Candied Ginger & Brandy Pound Cake

❧ ◆ ❧

The surprise of candied ginger and the hint of brandy combine to make a flavor that is different from any other pound cake you're likely to find. It's delicious!

1 cup (2 sticks) butter, room temperature
1-1/2 cups sugar
5 large eggs, room temperature
2-1/2 cups cake flour
2-1/2 teaspoons dried ginger
1/4 teaspoon salt
1/2 cup cream, room temperature
1/3 cup brandy
1 cup small diced crystallized ginger (about 20 large pieces) ✲
1-1/2 teaspoons orange extract

Preheat oven to 325 degrees.

Butter and flour a 9-1/2-inch bundt pan.

Cream together the butter and sugar until light and fluffy.

Add the eggs to the batter, one at a time, beating well after each addition.

In a bowl, whisk together the cake flour, ginger, and salt.

Add 1/2 of the flour to the batter. Then add the 1/2 cup cream. Gently but thoroughly blend in the remaining flour.

Fold in the brandy, chopped ginger, and orange extract. (Be sure to fold in thoroughly, but do not overbeat.)

Pour the batter into the prepared pan and bake at 325 degrees for 50-60 minutes, or until a tester comes out clean.

* *Note:* Crystallized ginger can be found at Williams Sonoma or other specialty cook stores and at most local farmers' markets.

Coffee Cake Pound Cake

∾ ✦ ∾

This is one of the all-time favorites among those who sampled the many cakes tested for this book. Coffee Cake Pound Cake can be served any time of the day, but it is a particular treat at brunch.

1 cup (2 sticks) butter, room temperature
2-1/4 cups sugar
3 large eggs, room temperature
1 cup sour cream, room temperature
1-1/4 teaspoons vanilla extract
2-1/2 cups cake flour
1/2 teaspoon baking powder
1/4 teaspoon baking soda
1/4 teaspoon salt

Topping:
6 tablespoons light brown sugar
1-1/2 teaspoons cinnamon
1 full cup chopped pecans

Preheat oven to 350 degrees.

Butter and flour a 9-1/2-inch bundt pan.

Cream the butter well, then slowly add the sugar and continue creaming the mixture at high speed for about 3 minutes. Add the eggs, one at a time, beating well after each addition.

Combine the sour cream and vanilla and then add to the batter. Sift the flour with the baking powder, baking soda, and salt. Mix the flour gently but thoroughly into the batter.

In a small bowl combine the topping ingredients.

Pour 1/2 the batter into the prepared bundt pan then sprinkle 2/3 of the topping mixture over the batter. Spread the remaining batter on top and sprinkle with the last 1/3 of the topping.

Bake in a 350-degree oven approximately 45-50 minutes.

Let cake cool in pan on a wire rack about 10-15 minutes then turn out cake and let it cool completely.

Pumpkin Pie Pound Cake

❦ ◆ ❦

This cake has all the seasonings and flavors associated with a traditional pumpkin pie, but it is a wonderful and welcome change from the ubiquitous dessert commonly served at Thanksgiving and Christmas.

1 cup Crisco
1 cup sugar
1/2 cup dark brown sugar
5 large eggs, room temperature
1 cup canned pumpkin
2-1/4 cups flour
2 teaspoons cinnamon
1 teaspoon freshly grated nutmeg
1/2 teaspoon mace
1/2 teaspoon salt
1 teaspoon baking soda
1/2 cup orange juice, room temperature
2 teaspoons vanilla
1-1/4 cups chopped pecans

Icing:

1 cup confectioners' sugar
4 tablespoons butter, melted
2 tablespoons orange juice
1/4 teaspoon orange extract

Preheat oven to 325 degrees.

Butter and flour a 10-1/2-inch decorative bundt pan.

Cream the shortening to lighten it, then gradually add both sugars, continuing to cream for about 5 minutes on high speed.

Add the eggs, one at a time, mixing well after each addition. Blend the pumpkin into the batter.

In a bowl, whisk together the flour, spices, salt, and baking soda, mixing well. Gradually beat the dry ingredients into the batter until well incorporated.

Fold in the orange juice, vanilla, and chopped pecans.

Pour the batter into the bundt pan, smoothing the top of the cake. Bake for 55-60 minutes, or until a tester comes out clean. Allow the cake to rest in the pan on a wire rack for 10-15 minutes; then turn out onto a rack and cool completely before icing.

For the **icing**, sift the confectioners' sugar, and then thoroughly mix with the remaining ingredients. Allow the icing to rest and thicken somewhat before icing the cooled cake. The icing will run down the sides of the cake when poured over the top.

Maple Syrup Pound Cake

❦ ✦ ❦

The light brushing of maple syrup on this still warm cake makes it very mellow and moist.

1-1/2 cups (3 sticks) butter, room temperature
1 cup sugar
5 large eggs, room temperature
3 cups flour, sifted
1/2 teaspoon baking powder
1 cup maple syrup, plus extra syrup for glaze
2 teaspoons vanilla extract
1/3 cup cream, room temperature

Preheat oven to 350 degrees.

Butter and flour a 9-inch bundt pan.

Cream together the butter and sugar. Add eggs, one at a time, beating slightly after each addition.

Sift together the flour and baking powder.

Combine the maple syrup, vanilla, and cream. Alternate the wet ingredients with the flour, beginning and ending with the flour.

Pour the batter into the bundt pan and bake at 350 degrees

for approximately 50 minutes, or until the cake tests done.

Let the cake sit in the pan for 10 to 15 minutes. Turn the cake out onto a rack. Brush the top of the still **warm** cake with the extra maple syrup, using only enough to make the cake glisten but not so much as to make it soggy.

SPECIAL NOTE: Remember that, unless noted otherwise in the recipe, *all refrigerated ingredients* (such as butter, eggs, milk, cream, sour cream, yogurt, etc.) should be brought to room temperature, but for no more than 1 hour. More than an hour of unrefrigerated time will cause the butter to become too soft and affect the success of the cake, and other items, such as eggs, may spoil.)

Bourbon Pecan Pound Cake

∽ ♦ ∾

1 cup (2 sticks) butter, room temperature
1 cup sugar
1-1/2 cups light brown sugar
5 large eggs, room temperature
2-3/4 cups flour
1/4 teaspoon salt
1 teaspoon baking powder
1/4 teaspoon mace
1/2 cup bourbon whiskey
1 teaspoon vanilla extract
1 teaspoon orange extract
1-1/2 cups chopped pecans

Preheat oven to 325 degrees.

Butter and flour a 10-inch tube pan.

Cream the softened butter until light, then gradually add both sugars and continue beating for about 5 minutes, incorporating as much air as possible into the batter.

Add the eggs, one at a time, mixing well after each addition.

Sift the flour with the salt, baking powder, and mace. Gradually add the four mixture to the batter. Fold in the bourbon, vanilla, and orange extract. Next, fold in the pecans.

Gently pour the batter into the prepared pan and smooth the top of the cake.

Bake in a 325-degree oven for about 1 hour, or until a tester comes out clean.

Cool in the pan on a wire rack for about 15 minutes, then turn out on a rack and cool the cake completely.

Coffee Kaluha Pound Cake

❧ ◆ ❧

The tastes in this cake are subtle, but accompany one another nicely. It is also a soft, sweet cake that keeps well when wrapped tightly with foil or plastic wrap.

1 cup (2 sticks) butter, room temperature
3 cups sugar
6 large eggs, room temperature
1 cup coffee yogurt, room temperature
1/4 teaspoon baking soda
1/4 teaspoon baking powder
1/4 teaspoon salt
3 cups sifted flour
3 tablespoons Kaluha
2 teaspoons instant espresso (or 1 tablespoon instant coffee) dissolved in 1 tablespoon boiling water
2 teaspoons vanilla extract

Preheat oven to 300 degrees.

Butter and flour a 9-1/2-inch bundt pan.

Cream the butter. Add sugar, one cup at a time, beating well after each addition.

Add eggs, one at a time, beating at medium speed after each addition. Add the coffee yogurt; beat well.

Add soda, baking powder and salt to the flour, and mix together with a wire whisk or fork. Add the dry ingredients to the batter, one cup at a time, mixing well after each addition. Add Kaluha, dissolved espresso, and vanilla extract. Mix well.

Pour into the prepared tube pan. Bake for 1 hour or until a cake tester comes out clean.

Let stand 10 minutes before removing from pan. Let cake cool completely on a rack before slicing.

Low Cholesterol Poppy Seed Pound Cake

❧ ◆ ❧

It's not easy to come up with a **pound cake** that is low in fat and low in cholesterol and still has any taste. But this light and airy cake, with the special flavor and texture of toasted poppy seeds, is a nice surprise for those who normally have to say no to baked goods.

PAM or other Non-Stick Cooking Spray
scant 1/4 cup poppy seeds
1/2 cup (1 stick) margarine, room temperature
3/4 cup granulated sugar
3 large egg whites, room temperature
1 tablespoon vanilla extract
3/4 teaspoon lemon extract
2-1/2 cups sifted cake flour
3/4 teaspoon baking soda
1/4 teaspoon salt
1 cup low-fat lemon yogurt, drained of any excess
liquid, room temperature
1-1/2 teaspoons finely grated lemon zest

Preheat oven to 325 degrees.

Spray the bottom and sides of a loaf pan that measures 8-1/2 x 4-1/2 inches and is approximately 3 inches deep. Dust lightly with flour and set aside.

In a dry, non-stick skillet, carefully toast the poppy seeds until lightly toasted and fragrant.

Cream together the margarine and sugar. Add egg whites and beat 4 minutes. Add vanilla and lemon extracts.

Combine the flour, soda, and salt.

Combine the yogurt and lemon zest.

Add the dry ingredients alternately with the yogurt, beginning and ending with the flour. Fold in the poppy seeds, being certain to incorporate well.

Pour into the prepared loaf pan and bake at 325 degrees for 40 to 55 minutes.

Note: be sure to check the cake at 40 minutes. Although in some ovens the cooking time may be longer, it is important not to overcook this cake as it will be too dry.

Let the cake rest in the pan for 5 to 10 minutes, then turn out onto a wire rack to cool.

Cheese Savory Pound Cake

❦ ◆ ❦

This savory, slightly sweet pound cake is perfect at tea time or served at a luncheon alongside a bowl of hot or cold soup or with a crisp, green salad.

1/2 cup lightly toasted pine nuts
1 cup (2 sticks) butter, room temperature
3/4 cup sugar
5 large eggs, room temperature
2 cups flour
1/2 teaspoon baking powder
1/4 teaspoon cayenne (red) pepper
1/4 cup milk, room temperature
1 cup grated sharp cheddar cheese
1/2 cup freshly grated Parmesan cheese

Preheat the oven to 350 degrees.

Butter and flour a 9-inch bundt pan.

Toast the pine nuts in a dry skillet, stirring constantly and watching closely to make sure they brown only enough to release their oils — about 2 to 3 minutes. Remove the pine nuts from the skillet and place in a small bowl. Set aside to cool.

Cream the softened butter. Gradually add the sugar, beating well. Continue beating another 3 to 4 minutes. Scrape the sides of the bowl and mix well.

Add the eggs, one at a time, mixing well after each addition.

Whisk together the flour, baking powder, and cayenne pepper. Add half the flour mixture to the batter, mixing well. Add the 1/4 cup milk, and follow with the remaining flour. Fold in (with a rubber spatula) the cheeses and cooled pine nuts. Scrape the sides of the bowl and stir.

Transfer the batter to the prepared bundt pan. Bake at 350 degrees for 35 to 40 minutes, or until a cake tester comes out clean.

Let the cake cool in the pan on a wire rack for 15 minutes. Unmold the cake and allow to cool completely.

Special Miniature Pound Cakes

Bittersweet & Orange Bundt-lette Pound Cakes

❧ ◆ ❧

Bundt-lette pans are made by Nordic Ware and are found at department stores and specialty cook shops. They make festive and attractive miniature pound cakes that can be wrapped decoratively and placed in gift baskets at Christmas or other special occasions. They also make perfect dinner-party desserts when surrounded by fresh fruit and whipped cream or ice cream.

Makes 14-16 mini pound cakes

Pam or Baker's Joy, or similar non-stick cooking spray
3/4 cup (1-1/2 sticks) butter, room temperature
1/2 cup Crisco
3 cups sugar
5 large eggs, room temperature
3 cups flour
1/4 teaspoon salt
1/2 teaspoon baking powder
1 cup milk, room temperature
6 ounces finely chopped bittersweet chocolate
1 tablespoon finely grated orange zest
1 teaspoon vanilla extract
1/2 teaspoon orange extract

Preheat oven to 325 degrees.

Spray Bundt-lettes with Baker's Joy or Pam. (This non-stick cooking spray is really needed; the traditional method of buttering and flouring the individual molds does not work well.)

Cream together the butter and Crisco on high speed until lightened in color, about 3 minutes. Gradually add the sugar and then continue beating for 5 minutes. Add the eggs, one at a time, beating well after each addition.

Whisk together the flour, salt, and baking powder. Add 1/3 of flour mixture to the batter, blend well, then add 1/2 cup of the milk, blending well again. Repeat with the remaining flour and milk.

Fold in the finely chopped chocolate, zest, and extracts.

Fill the Bundt-lette molds with the batter, coming to within 1/2-inch from the top. (If they are over-filled, they will overflow.)

Bake at 325 degrees for about 30 minutes, or until tested done.

Note: The Bundt-lettes will not brown on the top, but when turned out of the pan, they will be a golden color and look like miniature pound cakes.

Cool in the pan for 5 minutes, then turn out onto a rack and cool completely.

Raspberry Buttermilk Bundt-lette Pound Cakes

∽ ♦ ∽

Makes 14-16 mini pound cakes

Pam, Baker's Joy, or other non-stick cooking spray
1 cup (2 sticks) butter, room temperature
2-1/2 cups sugar
6 large eggs, room temperature
2-3/4 cups flour
1/4 teaspoon salt
3/4 teaspoon baking soda
1 cup buttermilk, room temperature
1 teaspoon finely grated orange zest
2 teaspoons finely grated lemon zest
1-1/2 teaspoons vanilla extract
1/2 teaspoon orange extract
fresh raspberries

Preheat oven to 325 degrees.

Spray the bundt-lette molds well with the non-stick cooking spray.

Cream the softened butter; slowly add the sugar and beat well, for 4 to 5 minutes.

Add the eggs, one at a time, beating well after each addition.

With a whisk, mix together the flour with the salt and baking soda. Alternately add the flour mixture and buttermilk.

Mix in the grated zests and extracts, combining well.

Carefully spoon into the bundt-lette molds, filling to half an inch from the top. (If they are over-filled, they will overflow.) Push into each mold 5 raspberries, sinking them just below the surface of the batter.

Bake at 325 degrees for 30 minutes.

Let the cakes sit in the pan on a wire rack for 5 minutes before unmolding. Unmold onto a wire rack and allow the bundt-lettes to cool completely. When cooled, wrap individually in foil or saran wrap for storage.

SPECIAL NOTE: Remember that, unless noted otherwise in the recipe, *all refrigerated ingredients* (such as butter, eggs, milk, cream, sour cream, yogurt, etc.) should be brought to room temperature, but for no more than 1 hour. More than an hour of unrefrigerated time will cause the butter to become too soft and affect the success of the cake, and other items, such as eggs, may spoil.)

Sour Cream Bundt-lette Pound Cakes

❧ ◆ ❧

Makes 14-16 mini pound cakes

Pam or Baker's Joy, or similar non-stick cooking spray
1 cup (2 sticks) butter, room temperature
1/2 cup Crisco
2-3/4 cups sugar
5 large eggs, room temperature
3 cups cake flour
1/4 teaspoon salt
1 teaspoon baking soda
1 cup sour cream, room temperature
1/4 cup milk, room temperature
1-1/2 teaspoons vanilla extract
1/2 teaspoon lemon extract
1 teaspoon orange extract

Preheat oven to 325 degrees.

Spray Bundt-lette molds with Baker's Joy or Pam. (This non-stick cooking spray is really needed; the traditional method of buttering and flouring the individual molds does not work well with the Bundt-lettes. Another hint: muffin tins do not work with this or the other mini pound cake recipes; therefore, the Nordic

Ware Bundt-lette pans are required if you plan to make these small cakes.)

Cream together butter and Crisco until lightened in color, about 3 minutes. Gradually add the sugar and then beat on high speed for 5 minutes. Add the eggs, one at a time, beating well after each addition.

Sift together the flour, salt, and soda; add one half of the dry ingredients to the batter.

Mix together the sour cream and milk and add to the batter, also blending well. Add the remaining flour mixture to the batter.

Gently mix in the vanilla, lemon, and orange extracts.

Pour batter into the individual molds, coming to within 1/2-inch of the top. (If they are over-filled, they will overflow.)

Bake at 325 degrees for about 30 minutes, or until they test done.

Cool in the pan for 5 minutes, then turn out on a rack and cool completely.

Currant Bundt-lette Pound Cakes

❧ ✦ ❧

Makes 14-16 mini pound cakes

Extra softened butter and sugar for preparing the pans
1 cup (2 sticks) butter, room temperature
1/2 cup Crisco
3 cups sugar
5 large eggs, room temperature
3 cups sifted flour
1 teaspoon baking powder
1/2 teaspoon salt
1 teaspoon allspice
1 cup milk, room temperature
1/2 teaspoon vanilla extract
1/2 cup currants

Preheat oven to 325 degrees.

Prepare the Bundt-lette pans by coating well with softened butter and then sprinkle with granulated sugar to coat well (the same as you would if you were dusting pans with flour.)

Cream butter, shortening, and sugar together. Add eggs, one at a time, stirring constantly. Sift flour, baking powder, salt, and allspice together.

Add dry ingredients to creamed mixture alternately with the milk. Add the vanilla extract.

Fold in the currants.

Fill the Bundt-lette molds with the batter, coming to within 1/2-inch from the top. (If they are over-filled, they will over-flow.)

Bake at 325 degrees for 30 to 35 minutes. Let the cakes sit in the pan on a wire rack for 5 minutes before unmolding. Unmold onto a wire rack and allow the bundt-lettes to cool completely. When cooled, wrap individually in foil or saran wrap for storage.

Glazed Chocolate Bundt-lette Pound Cakes

❧ ◆ ☙

The smooth, rich chocolate glaze that is drizzled over these small pound cakes makes them irresistible.

Makes 16-18 mini pound cakes

Pam, Baker's Joy, or other non-stick cooking spray
2 cups (4 sticks) butter, room temperature
3 cups sugar
6 large eggs, room temperature
3-1/2 cups flour
1 teaspoon baking soda
1/4 teaspoon salt
1/2 cup cocoa
1 cup sour cream, room temperature
1 tablespoon vanilla extract

Chocolate Glaze:
6 ounces bittersweet chocolate
3 tablespoons cream
1 tablespoon water
3 tablespoons butter

Preheat oven to 325 degrees.

Spray the Bundt-lette pans with the non-stick cooking spray (the traditional method of buttering and flouring the pans does not work well in these pans).

Cream the softened butter. Gradually add the sugar and beat well. Add the eggs, one at a time, mixing well after each addition.

Whisk together the flour, baking soda, salt, and cocoa. Add half of the flour mixture to the batter and mix. Add the sour cream. And finally add the last half of the flour mixture. Incorporate well, but do not overbeat.

Pour into the prepared pans and bake at 325 degrees for 25 to 30 minutes, being careful not to overcook. Let the cakes rest in the pans for 5 minutes, then turn out onto a wire rack. When the cakes are completely cooled, drizzle with the chocolate glaze.

To make the **glaze**, melt the bittersweet chocolate with the other ingredients in a small saucepan over low heat. Drizzle the melted chocolate over the top of each bundt-lette, allowing the glaze to drip down the sides of the cake. When the cakes are iced, they must be refrigerated, well-covered. They are at their best, though, when allowed to return to room temperature before serving.

Index

Candied Orange
Candied Orange Pound Cake 14
Candied Orange Rind 15

Caramel
Caramel Sauce to go with Toasted Pecan and Brown Sugar Pound Cake 60

Cheddar
Cheese Savory Pound Cake 76

Cheese
Cheese Savory Pound Cake 76
Apricot, CreamCheese, and Walnut pound Cake 19
Lemon Cream Cheese Pound Cake 46
Raspberry Swirl Pound Cake 2

Cherries
Fresh Cherry Pound Cake 4

Chocolate
Bittersweet and Orange Bundt-lette Pound Cake 80
Buttermilk Chocolate Pound Cake 26
Chocolate Chip Cookie Pound Cake 30
Chocolate Glaze 88
Chocolate Truffle Pound Cake 37
Chocolate Walnut Pound Cake 28
Glazed Chocolate Bundt-lette Pound Cakes 88
Mocha Pound Cake with Coffee Creme Anglaise 34
Oreo Pound Cake 32

Christmas
Cranberry Walnut Pound Cake 23
Bourbon Pecan Pound Cake 70

Coconut
Coconut Pound Cake 8

Coffee
Coffee Cake Pound Cake 64
Coffee Creme Anglaise 35
Coffee Kaluha Pound Cake 72
Mocha Pound Cake 34

Cookies
Chocolate Chip Cookie Pound Cake 30
Oreo Pound Cake 32

Cornmeal
Southern Chess Pound Cake 58

Cranberry
Cranberry Walnut Pound Cake 23

Cream
Apple Ginger Pound Cake 16
Candied Ginger and Brandy Pound Cake 62
Caramel Sauce 60
Chocolate Glaze 88
French Vanilla Pound Cake 42
Maple Syrup Pound Cake 68
Oreo Pound Cake 32
Pistachio Pound Cake 54
Spiced Whipped Cream 57

Cream Cheese
  Apricot, Cream Cheese, and
    Walnut Pound Cake 19
  Lemon Cream Cheese Pound Cake 46
  Raspberry Swirl Pound Cake 2

Currants
  Currant Bundt-lette Pound Cakes 86

Fruit
  Apple Ginger Pound Cake 16
  Apricot, Cream Cheese, and
    Walnut Pound Cake 19
  Candied Orange Pound Cake 14
  Coconut Pound Cake 8
  Cranberry Walnut Pound Cake 23
  Currant Bundt-lette Pound Cakes 86
  Fresh Cherry Pound Cake 4
  Glazed Banana Pound Cake 10
  Grandmother Bibb's Prune Pound
    Cake 21
  Lemon Cream Cheese Pound Cake 46
  Pineapple-Macadamia Nut Pound
    Cake 6
  Raspberry Buttermilk Bundt-lette
    Pound Cakes 82
  Raspberry Swirl Pound Cake 2
  Summer Blueberry Pound Cake 12
  Susan's Orange Pound Cake 40

Ginger
  Apple Ginger Pound Cake with
    Custard Sauce 16
  Candied Ginger and Brandy Pound
    Cake 62

Glazes
  Glazed Banana Pound Cake 10
  Glazed Chocolate Bundt-lette
    Pound Cakes 88

Kaluha
  Coffee Kaluha Pound Cake 72

Lemon
  Lemon Cream Cheese Pound Cake 46
  Lemon Glaze 47

Loaf Pound Cakes
  Apple Ginger Pound Cake with
    Custard Sauce 16
  Candied Orange Pound Cake 14
  Half-A-Pound Cake 49
  Liza's Pound Cake 44
  Low Cholesterol Poppy Seed
    Pound Cake 74
  Susan's Orange Pound Cake 40

Low-cholesterol
  Low Cholesterol Poppy Seed
    Pound Cake 74

Low-fat
  Low Cholesterol Poppy Seed
    Pound Cake 74

Macadamia Nuts
  Pineapple-Macadamia Nut Pound
    Cake 6

Maple Syrup
  Maple Syrup Pound Cake 68

Coffee Creme Anglaise, with Mocha
Pound Cake 35
Custard Sauce, with Apple Ginger
Pound Cake 16
Lemon Glaze, with Lemon Cream
Cheese Pound Cake 47

Savory
Cheese Savory Pound Cake 76

Sour Cream
Chocolate Chip Cookie Pound Cake
30
Coffee Cake Pound Cake 64
Glazed Banana Pound Cake 10
Glazed Chocolate Bundt-lette
Pound Cakes 88
Liza's Pound Cake 44
Sour Cream Bundt-lette Pound
Cakes 84
Toasted Pecan and Brown Sugar
Pound Cake 60

Springform pan
for baking Lemon Cream Cheese
Pound Cake 46

Sweet Potatoes
Sweet Potato Pound Cake 56

Syrup
Maple Syrup Pound Cake 68

Vanilla
French Vanilla Pound Cake 42

Vanilla Bean in:
French Vanilla Pound Cake 42
Pineapple-Macadamia Nut Pound
Cake 6

Yogurt
Coffee Yogurt, in Coffee Kaluha
Pound Cake 72
Coffee Yogurt, in Mocha Pound
Cake 34
Lemon Yogurt, in Low Choles-
terol Poppy Seed Pound Cake 74
Vanilla Yogurt, in Chocolate Walnut
Pound Cake 28

Walnuts
Apricot, Cream Cheese, and
Walnut Pound Cake 19
Chocolate Walnut Pound Cake 28
Cranberry Walnut Pound Cake 23
Grandmother Bibb's Prune Pound
Cake with Walnut Icing 21